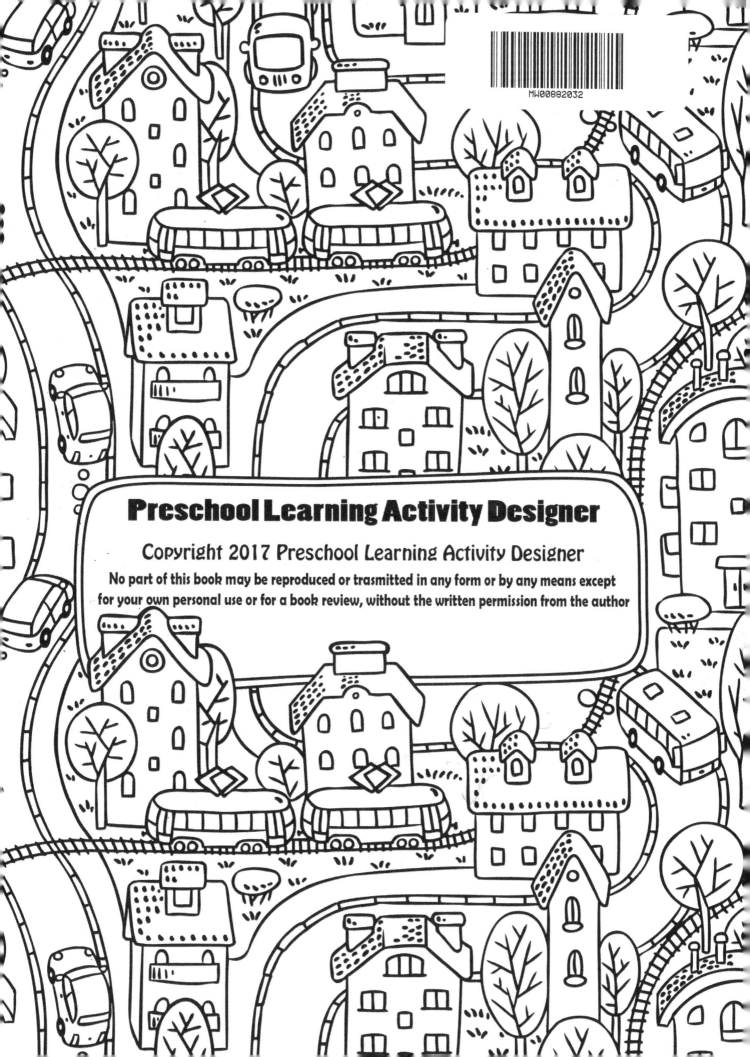

Preschool Learning Activity Designer

MW00882032

THIS BOOK BELONG TO

....

Find the Correct Shadow

Find Hidden Word

Maze Game

Find Hidden Word

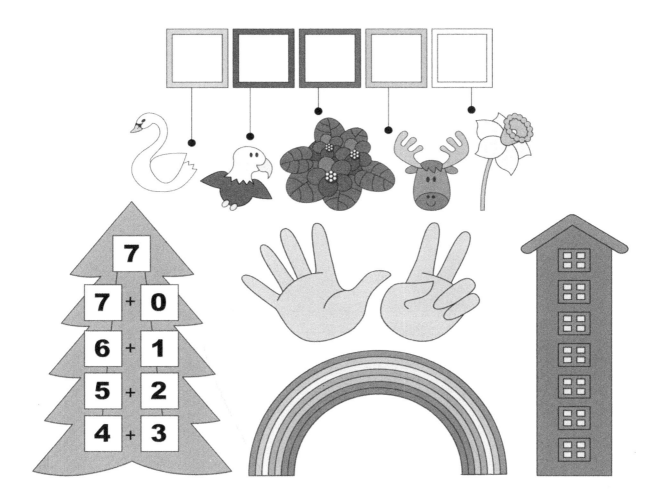

Matching Game

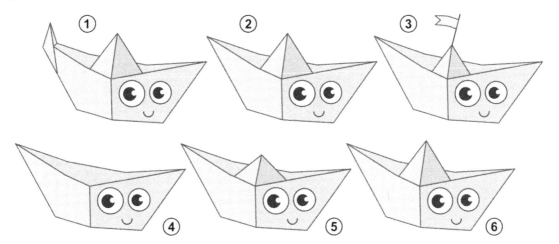

Find Hidden Word

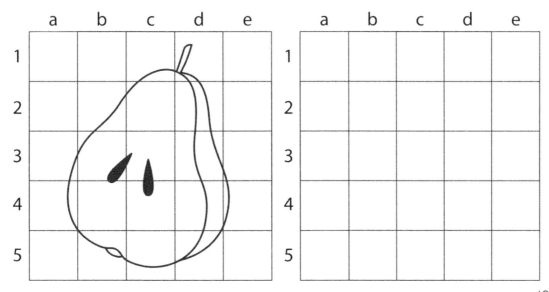

Find Hidden Word

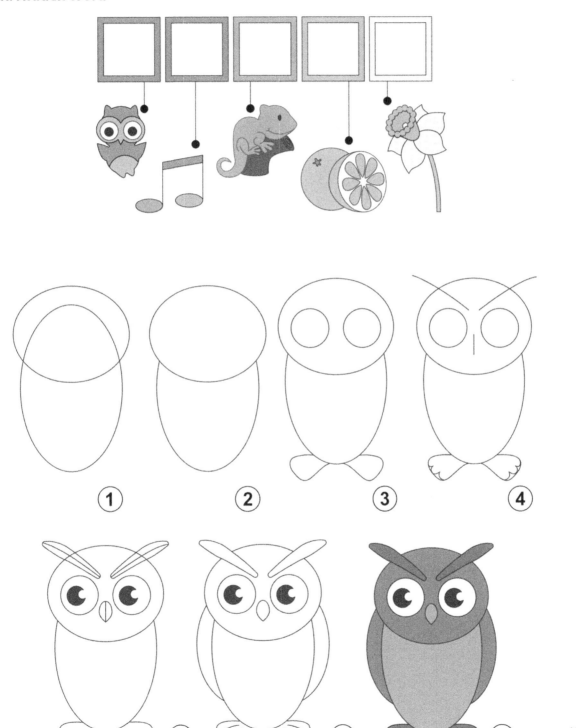

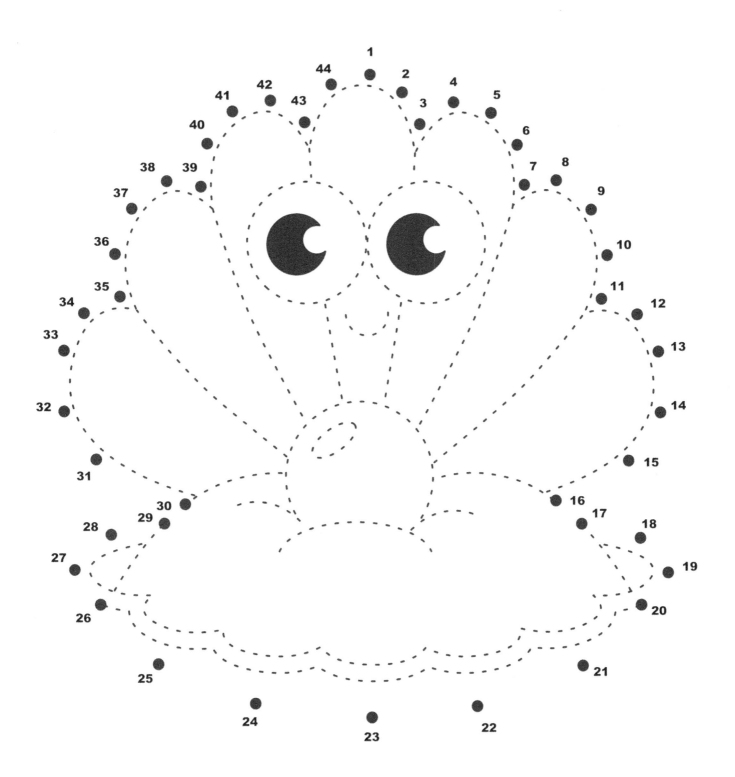

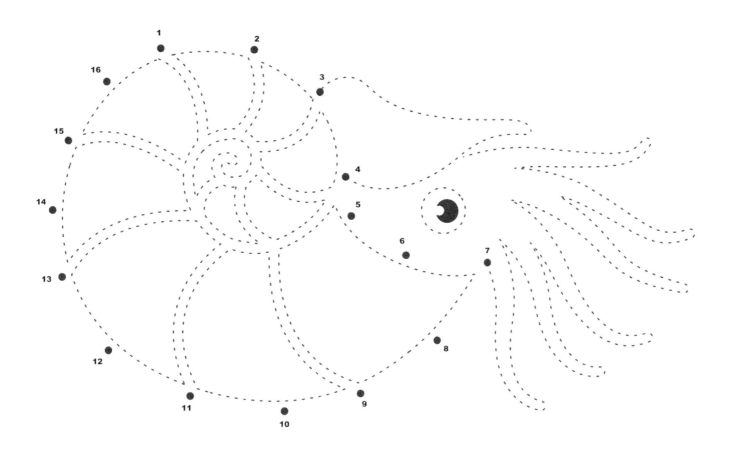

Find Hidden Word

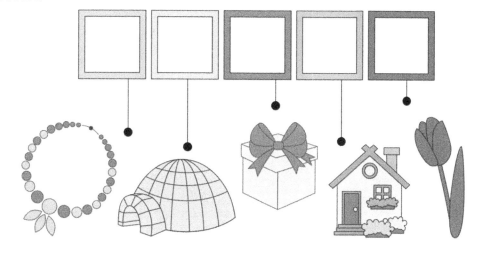

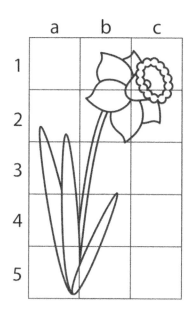

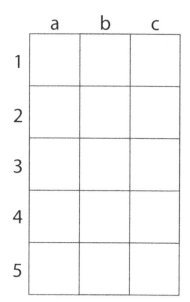

Find the Correct Shadow

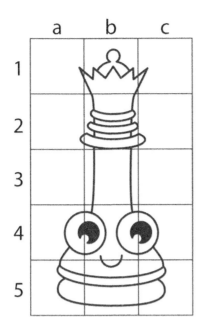

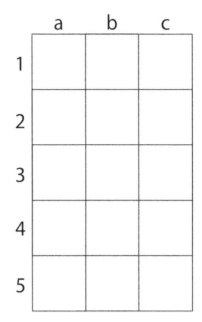

Find Hidden Word

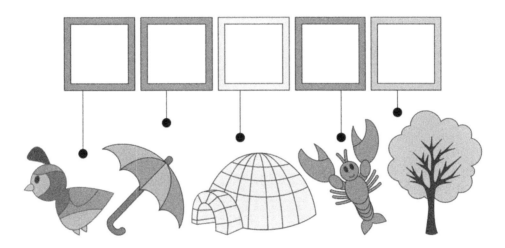

Matching Game

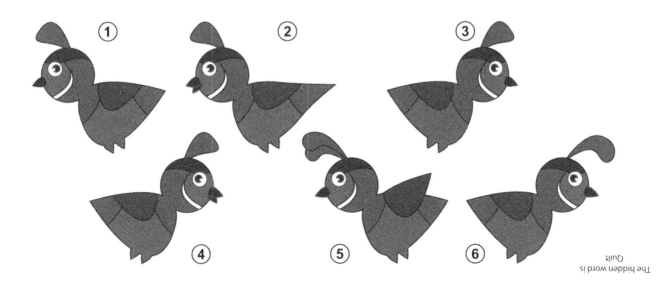

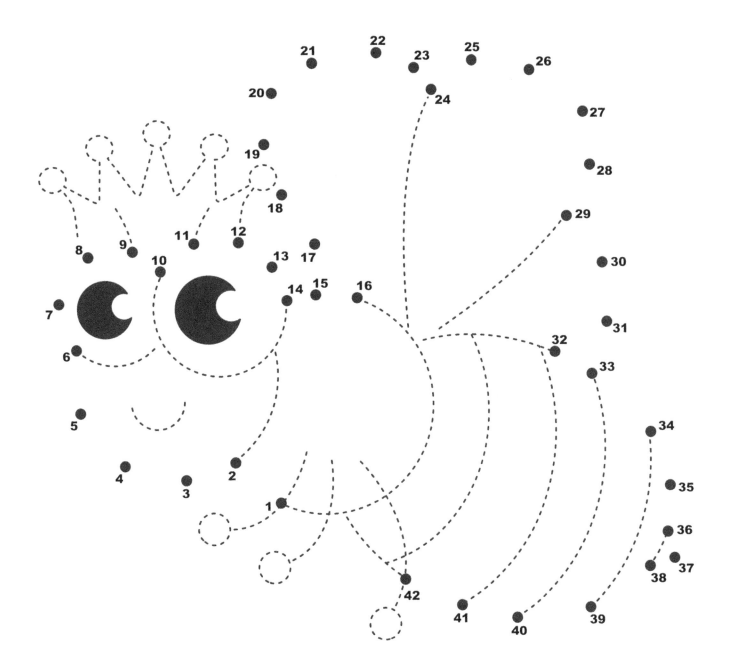

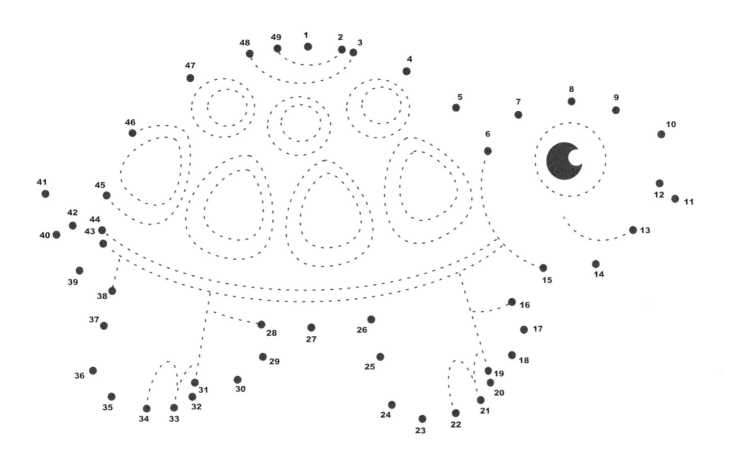

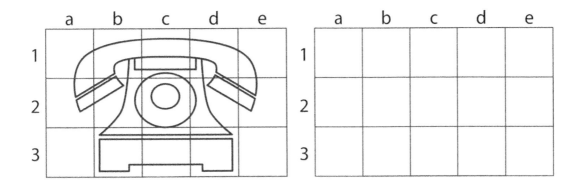

Find Hidden Word

Maze Game

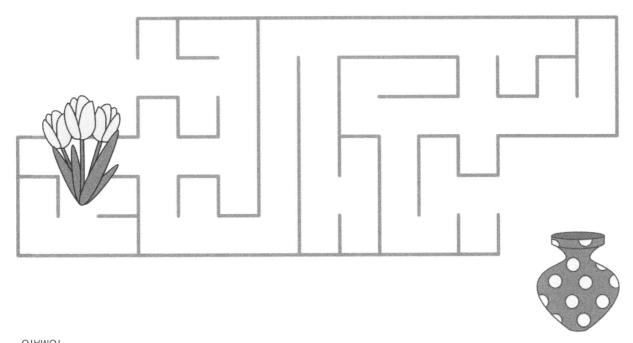

Connect the dots

1 ·
2 ·
46 ·
41 ·
40 ·
42 ·
45 ·
3 ·
39 ·
38 ·
37 ·
44 ·
43 ·
4 ·
5 ·
36 ·
6 ·
34 ·
35 ·
33 ·
7 ·
32 ·
30 · 31 ·
29 ·
28 ·
27 ·
8 ·
9 ·
10 ·
26 ·
11 ·
25 ·
24 ·
12 ·
13 ·
14 ·
23 ·
18 ·
19 ·
15 ·
22 ·
21 ·
20 ·
17 ·
16 ·

R R R R R R R

R

R

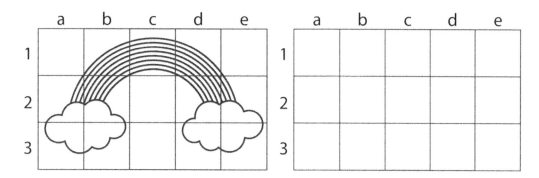

Find Hidden Word

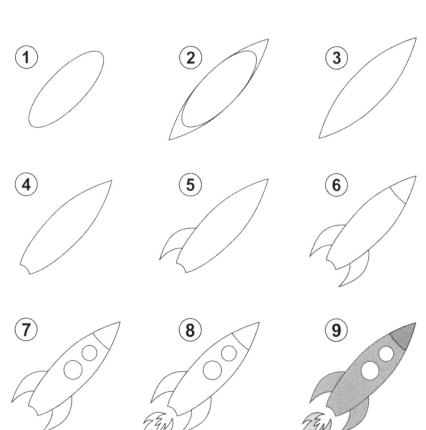

Connect the dots

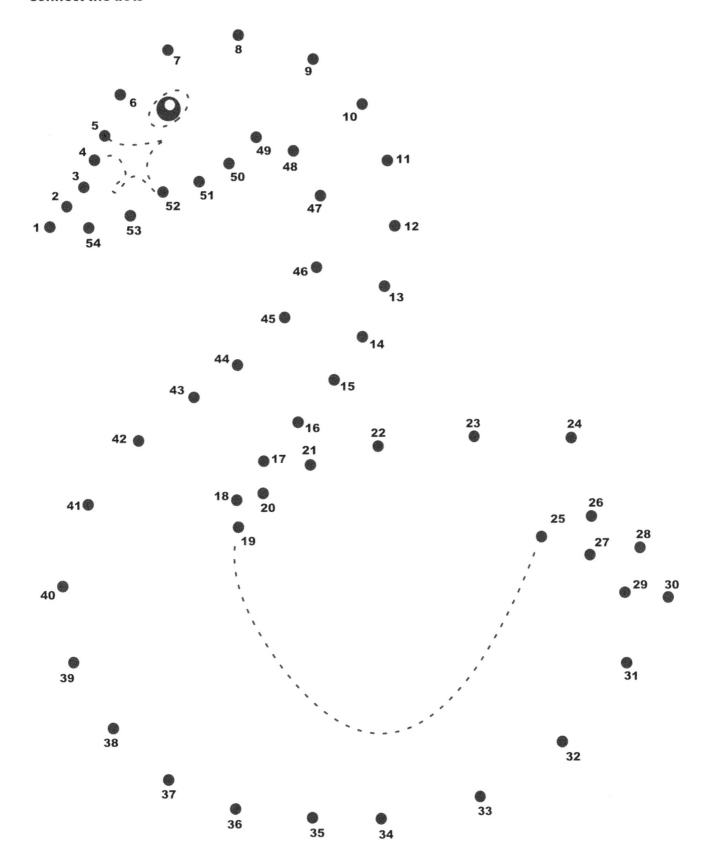

Matching Game

Find Hidden Word

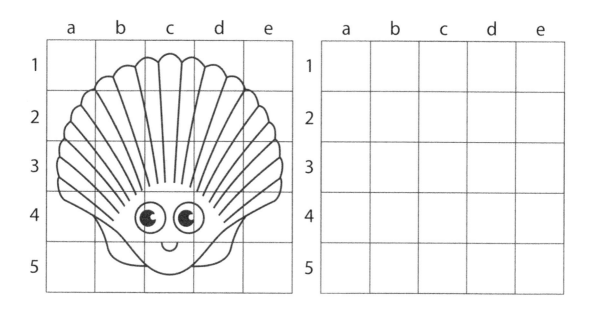

Connect the dots

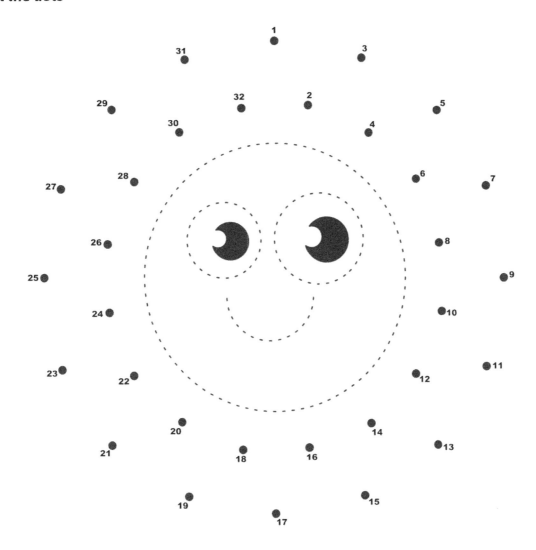

Find the Correct Shadow

Find the Correct Shadow

Maze Game

Connect the dots

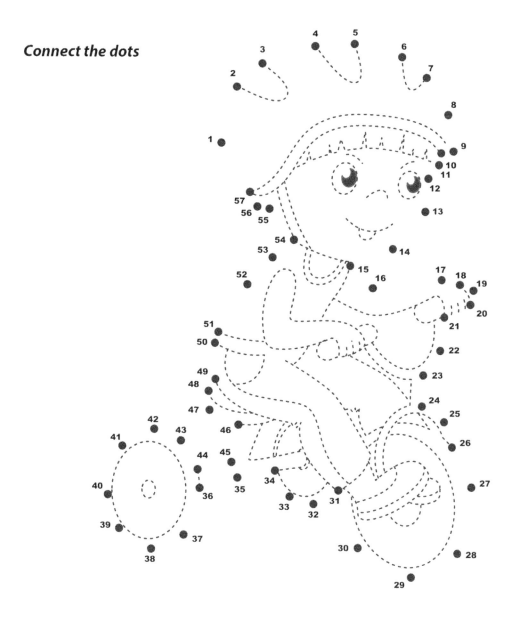

Find Hidden Word

Maze Game

Connect the dots

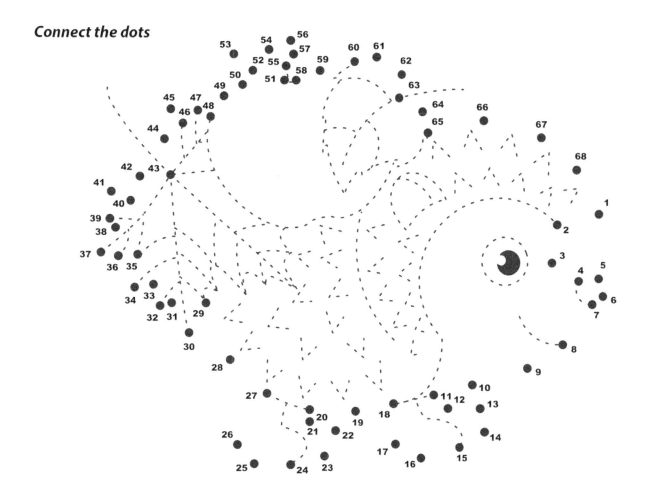

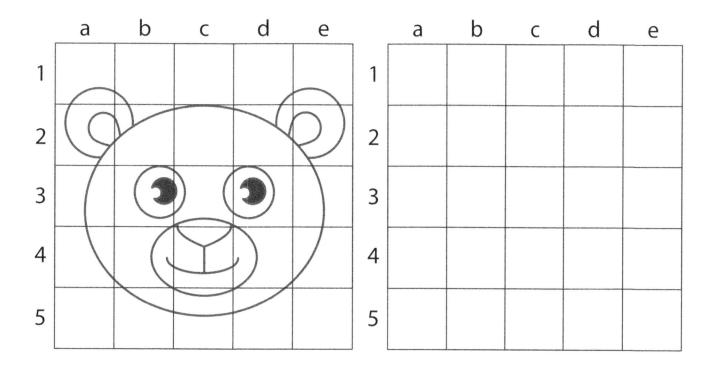

Find Hidden Word

Find the Correct Shadow

Maze Game

Connect the dots

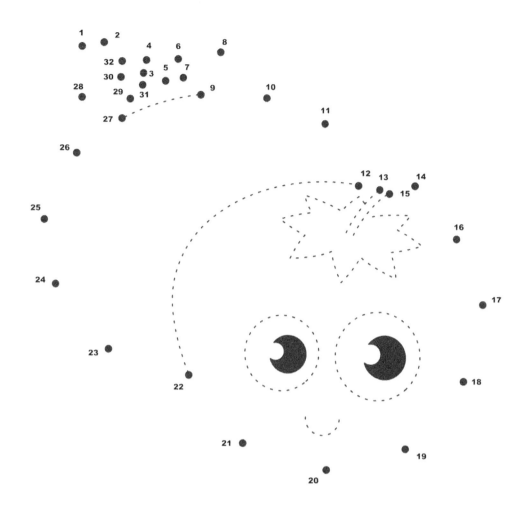

Find Hidden Word

Maze Game

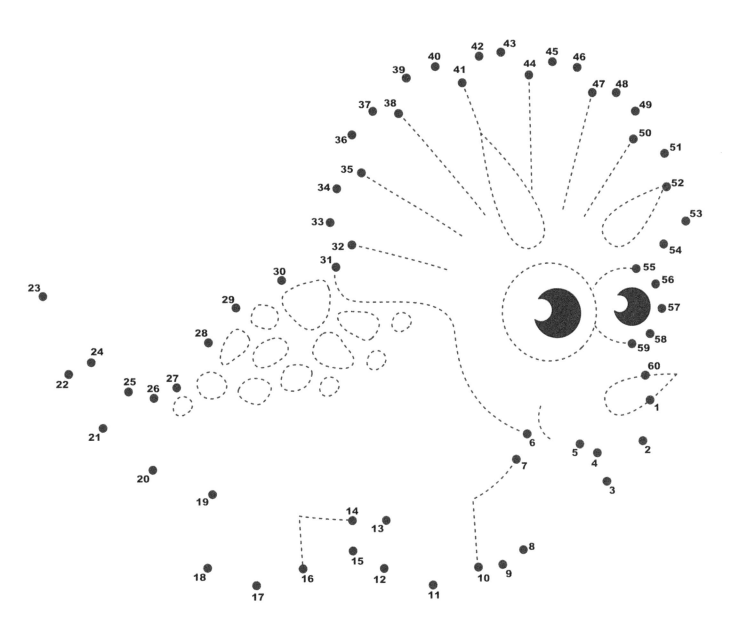

Tracing Game

Connect the dots

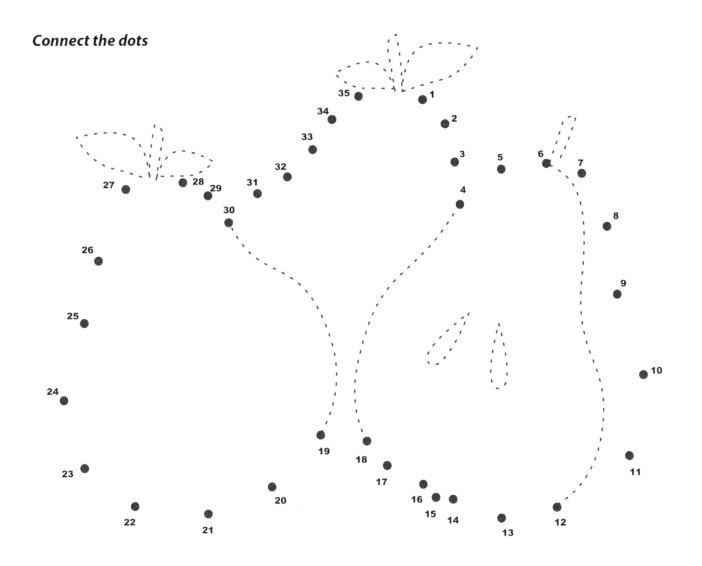

Find Hidden Word

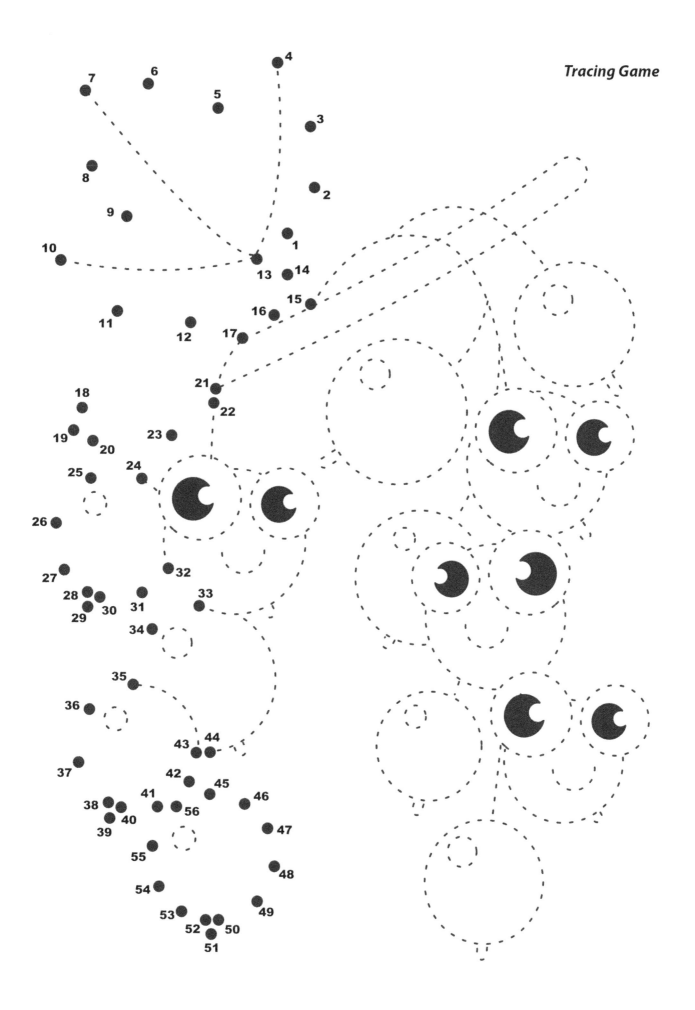

Find the Correct Shadow

Maze Game

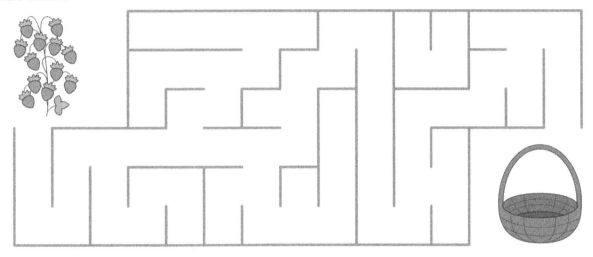

Find Hidden Word

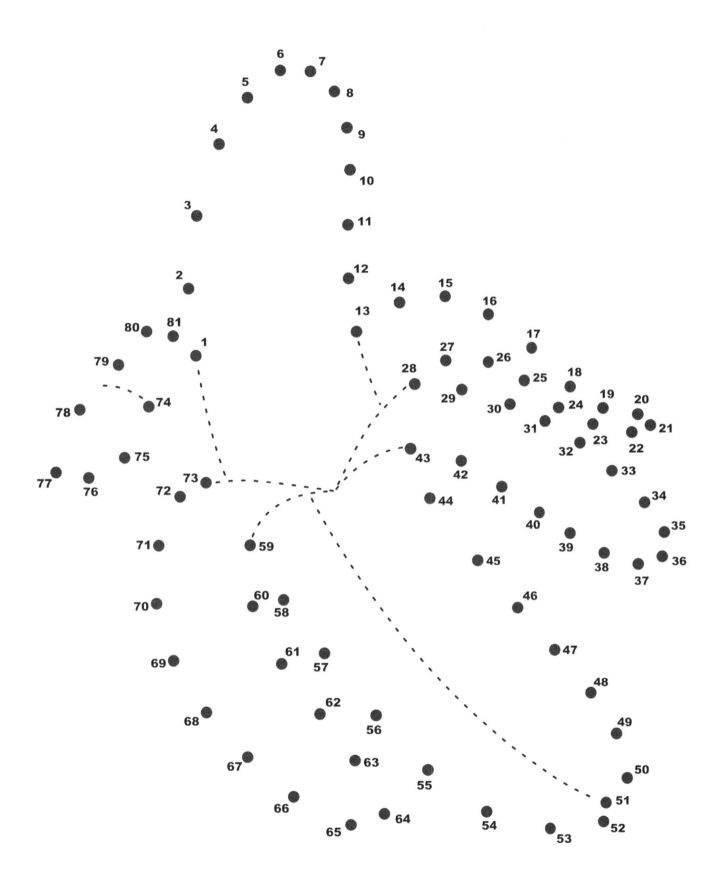

Matching Game

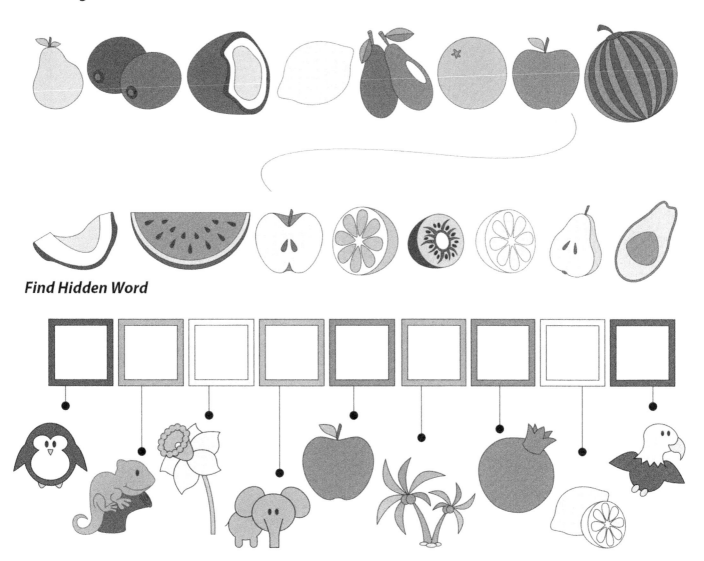

Find Hidden Word

Maze Game

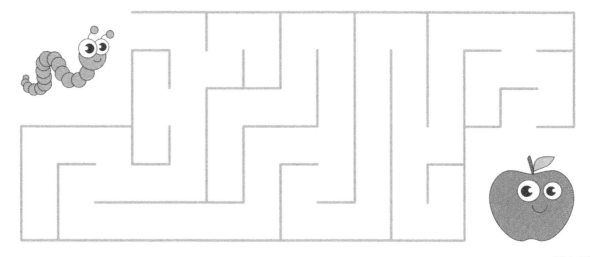

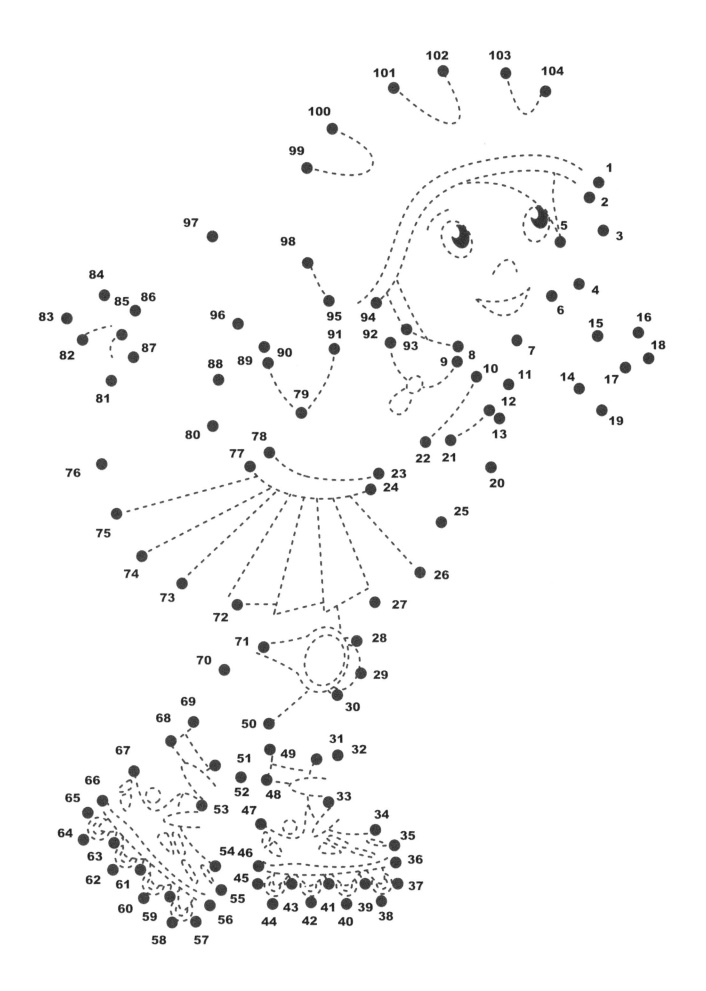

Find Hidden Word

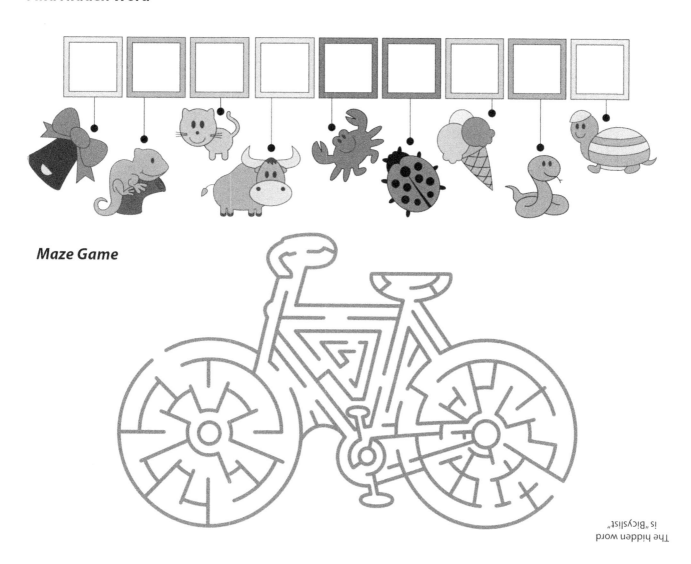

Maze Game

Made in the USA
Middletown, DE
13 December 2018